JONAH

WHEN GOD CHANGES

Topical Line Drives
Volume 24

BRUCE G. EPPERLY

Energion Publications
Gonzalez, FL
2016

Unless otherwise annotated, scripture quotations are from the New Revised Standard Version of the Bible (NRSV), copyright © 1989 by the Division of the Christian Education of the National Council of the Churches of Christ in the USA.

ISBN10: 1-63199-293-7
ISBN13: 978-1-63199-293-3

Energion Publications
P. O. Box 841
Gonzalez, FL 32560

energion.com

TABLE OF CONTENTS

CHAPTER ONE
WHEN GOD CHANGES THE RULES

What would you do if God asked you to challenge everything you thought was true? What if God told you to turn your back on the religious values you learned in church and in the Bible? What if God also urged you to go into the heart of darkness, the enemy camp, preaching a word of condemnation that might just lead to salvation for the oppressor? Worse yet, what if God changed God's mind to expand the circle of grace to include our nation's worst enemies, let's say, al Qaeda, ISIS, and the Taliban? What would you do? Would you go willingly on a mission trip to Nineveh or occupied Iraq or Syria?

Moreover, what if the God you believed in, the God whose biblical message was clear and authoritative, changed the rules of the faith, threw out the spiritual guidebook that shaped your life, and commanded you to adopt a different, and unprecedented, approach to life? Would you follow God's new directions, stay put, or run away from this rule-changing God? In the pages ahead, you will discover that this is the heart of Jonah's message.

In the past few decades, committed Christians have struggled with theologically radical ways of reconceiving marriage and divorce, equal rights, war and peace, the insights of other religions, homosexuality and marriage equality, and the nature of mission in light of changing understandings of God's vision for our world. If God is still speaking, then God can surprise us with new insights for changing times. Like Jonah, we must decide how we will respond to a god whose ways are different than we imagined.

The Book of Jonah is a radical story, inviting us to consider how we would respond if God asked us to disobey what we've always known to be true, and disregard what we previously believed were God's own words. The philosopher Alfred North Whitehead describes the worship of God as an adventure of the spirit and Jonah is thrust, against his will, into a profound spiritual adventure. This utterly confused prophet doesn't know where God is leading him or what God wants from him. So enamored of orthodox understandings of God's ways, he cannot imagine that his Creator is the God of novelty as well as tradition.

In a world in which politicians fan the flames of fear and anger, Jonah presents a provocative possibility: What if God loves our enemies as much as God loves our friends? What if God's revelation comes to outsiders as well as persons from our own faith tradition? Such inclusive thinking got Jesus in trouble following his first sermon and it caused Jonah to flee from the presence of God. Following Jesus' first sermon in his hometown Nazareth, the crowd is amazed at Jesus' reading from the prophet Isaiah:

> The Spirit of the Lord is upon me,
> because he has anointed me
> to bring good news to the poor.
> He has sent me to proclaim release to the captives
> and recovery of sight to the blind,
> to let the oppressed go free,
> to proclaim the year of the Lord's favor. (Luke 4:18-19)

In the blink of an eye, the hometown crowd turns on Jesus, when he has the audacity, and dare we say chutzpah, to claim that divine providence embraces friend and foe, and neighbor and stranger alike:

> But the truth is, there were many widows in Israel in the
> time of Elijah, when the heaven was shut up three years and
> six months, and there was a severe famine over all the land; yet
> Elijah was sent to none of them except to a widow at Zarephath
> in Sidon. There were also many lepers in Israel in the time
> of the prophet Elisha, and none of them was cleansed except
> Naaman the Syrian. (Luke 4:25-27)

When God changes the rules which undergird our way of life and then welcomes outsiders into God's inner circle, all hell breaks loose. Jesus' listeners want to throw him off a cliff and Jonah wants to flee to the outermost territories of the earth.

We are all tempted to create a God of our own making, who will uphold the status quo and baptize our values as God's definitive word. When God challenges our way of life and the religious and cultural values we hold dear, we are tempted to run away in search a new god — a god of our own making — who will support our privileges and prejudices and lead us into battle against our foes. In contrast to nationalist and parochial images of God, the Book of Jonah portrays a different vision of God: God, the iconoclast; God, the lover of our enemies; and God, who cares for non-humans with the same devotion as God cares for humankind. Constantly doing a new thing, God calls us to be innovative and iconoclastic as we embrace new understandings of God's vision for humankind and the world.

Jonah is a radical text and my interpretation is equally radical. I believe that Jonah's flight results from his experience of theological cognitive dissonance, the tension he experiences when God appears to overturn God's previous mandates and expand the scope of Jonah's prophetic vocation to include enemies of his nation. Jonah doesn't believe he is disobedient. In fact, his disobedience results from what Terence Fretheim describes as a "certain belief that he has."[1] He believes that God changed God's mind, and he doesn't know which way to go. His running away is a running from a new, more universal and loving, vision of God. Fretheim continues: "The issue in the book then is the issue between a man of faith and his God. It is an issue that involves an *interpretation* of an aspect of the meaning of that relationship. It is a *theological conflict*."[2]

Today, we hear the chorus, "Black lives matter!" in light of the USA's institutionalized racism, infecting even our law enforcement agencies. Many white Christians can't imagine that they are part of a racist system that requires radical economic and judicial transformation. Jonah hears an equally radical word, "Ninevite lives matter!" despite the enmity of Israel and Assyria and Nineveh's role in destroying the Northern Kingdom of Israel.

Jonah is a mysterious text that poses equally difficult ethical and theological questions that no politician wants to face and few religious leaders want to address. But, address them we must! Fidelity to God, human survival, and the soul of our nation demands it. Does God love the non-human world with the same ardor as

1 Terence Fretheim, *The Message of Jonah: A Theological Commentary* (Eugene: OR: Wipf and Stock, 2000), 19.
2 Ibid., 19.

3

God loves us? Does God call us to love the ISIS terrorists and welcome Syrian immigrants as well as to care for the world around us,
both its living creatures and its natural resources? These questions
may not dictate domestic or foreign policy but they serve as a lens
through which persons of faith must view the messy political and
social issues of our time.

Perhaps, in the Book of Jonah, we see the prefiguring of Jesus'
challenge to love our neighbor as ourselves, his embrace of his nation's enemies, his invitation to radical inclusion in the Sermon on
the Mount, and his open table to sinners and outsiders. The Book
of Jonah invites us to take a spiritual journey, whether or not we
leave our own hometown. Jonah asks us what it means to follow
God's way in a world of terrorism, xenophobia (fear of strangers), and fear-based politics. God calls us toward world-changing
discipleship in our time. Will we run away from God's vision or
follow God's call to embrace otherness, with all our ambivalence
and anxiety, or will we baptize our prejudice and hatred in the
waters of religious faith?

A Word of Thanks. I want to give thanks to the members of
my Sunday morning Bible Study class at South Congregational
Church, United Church of Christ, in Centerville, Massachusetts
for their interest, openness, and desire to grow in faith. This study
emerged out of a three-session series in February 2016. I am bless-
ed to be pastor of a congregation where spiritual growth, biblical
study, and faith formation is at the heart of its mission. I want to
thank Patricia Adams Farmer, Jan Fletcher, and Chris Twyeffort,
who read and commented on the text. I also wish to thank Terence
Fretheim for his insightful and innovative text, *The Message of Jonah.* His insights as a biblical scholar complemented and enriched
my theological approach to the Book of Jonah. I pray that as you
read this text your own world will open up to embrace unexpected
companions in God's journey of Shalom.

CHAPTER TWO
A WHALE OF A STORY?

I grew up watching the television show "Dragnet." It's still one of my favorites and on occasion I still tune into cable television to follow the exploits of Detective Sergeant Joe Friday as he seeks to apprehend some of Los Angeles' most notorious criminals. A hallmark of Friday's style involves his invocation "Just the facts, ma'am" whenever someone he's questioning begins to ramble, go off topic, or suggest a fantastic explanation for a crime he or she has observed. For Friday, the facts are everything. There is no room for vagueness, poetry, or speculation.

This same fact-based approach is true for many Christians. When they read the Bible, they assume that everything happened just as reported. Any hint of poetry, legend, or myth places the veracity of a particular text or the whole biblical witness at risk. To suggest any point of contact with pagan folk tales or assert that certain biblical stories are fictional is to doubt God's own integrity. As one bumper sticker proclaims, "The Bible says it. I believe it, and that settles it!" To question the factuality of the Book of Jonah — whether a character like Jonah actually lived, was swallowed by a big fish, or preached to the real citizens of a real Nineveh — is an act of impiety and challenge to God's word and wisdom. After all, the literalist asserts, if you can't trust the factuality of Jonah and its tale of a friendly fish, the factuality of the crucifixion and resurrection are also subject to doubt.

As I seek to fathom the Book of Jonah, I follow the wisdom of the philosopher Alfred North Whitehead who noted that although factuality is important, "it is more important that a proposition be interesting than true." The Book of Jonah presents us with a provocative and interesting proposition, "God can change God's mind, reverse God's previous positions, and embrace the enemy while chiding God's chosen ones." The Book of Jonah is a folk tale, but it is more than a literary bagatelle or amusing story. Jonah is a playful and artistic window into God's care for humankind and the non-human world.

An interested reader might begin with the question, "Who is Jonah and what do we know about him?" Much to Joe Friday's and the biblical literalist's chagrin, the only proper response is "virtually nothing." Apart from this short text of four chapters and forty eight verses, the name "Jonah" appears in only one other biblical passage and this passage says nothing about a prophetic journey to Nineveh, a storm at sea, or a miraculous fish. According to 2 Kings 14:24, in the 8th century BCE, the ethically ambiguous King Jeroboam II of Israel "restored the border of Israel from Lebo-hamath as far as the Sea of the Arabah, according to the word of the LORD, the God of Israel, which he spoke by his servant Jonah son of Amittai, the prophet, who was from Gath-hepher." Scholars note that the name Amittai means "faithfulness" or "truthfulness," while the name Jonah means "dove," a term often applied to the people of Israel (Hosea 7:11; 11:11; Psalm 74:19).

The curious reader will also be thwarted as he or she attempts to fathom when, where, or to whom the Book of Jonah was written. Some scholars suggest that the Book of Jonah was written between the sixth and fourth century BCE, but the exact occasion and audience are unknown. They suggest that its vague description of the city of Nineveh implies that the book was written after the destruction of Nineveh in 612 BCE. Perhaps, the Book of Jonah was written to counter the nationalism and xenophobia that surfaced in the time following the return of the Jewish nation from captivity in Babylon. (538 BCE) The Assyrians, whose capital was Nineveh, were hated by the Jews. As God's instruments of wrath, they had defeated the Northern Kingdom, Israel, and carried its citizens into exile (2 Kings 15:29; 18:9-12). Assyrian soldiers under the leadership of King Sennacherib marched to the gates of Jerusalem, the capital of the Southern Kingdom, Judah, and, apart from divine intervention, would have conquered the city. According to legend, God killed 185,000 Assyrian soldiers in one night to secure the freedom of Jerusalem (Isaiah 37:38).

It was clear to any right thinking Jew that God hated Assyria, and so should the Jewish people. God showed no mercy to the

Assyrian soldiers and neither should we! Nationalism and theological orthodoxy demanded that while God will save Jerusalem, Nineveh is outside the scope of God's loving providence. Still, the Book of Jonah is full of surprises and the ten minutes it takes to read the book may change your understanding of God's character and action in the world.

CHAPTER THREE
JONAH'S PERILOUS ADVENTURE
(JONAH 1:1-17)

What would you do if God upset everything you believed and turned your world upside down with an unexpected and undesirable mystical experience?

Many people think moments of illumination and inspiration are, by definition, comforting. In reality, nothing could be further from the truth. In the biblical tradition, encounters with God and God's messengers are almost always unsettling. When the angels come to Mary, Joseph and the shepherds, their first word to them is "Don't be afraid." Isaiah confesses his sinfulness when encounters God in the Temple (Isaiah 6:1-8). Peter stammers "go away from me, Lord, for I am a sinful man" after Jesus produces a miraculous catch of fish (Luke 5:1-11). In his *The Lion, The Witch, and the Wardrobe*, C.S. Lewis describes Susan's queries regarding the Great King Aslan. "Ooh" said Susan. "I'd thought he was a man. Is he quite safe? I shall feel rather nervous about meeting a lion"..."Safe?" said Mr. Beaver. "Who said anything about safe? 'Course he isn't safe. But he's good. He's the King, I tell you."

The Meaning of Revelation. The first words of the Book of Jonah are the "word of God came to Jonah the son of Amittai, saying 'Go at once to Nineveh, the great city, and cry out against it; for their wickedness has come up before me" (1:1). "The word of God came" is a common description of the prophetic call (Hosea 1:1; Joel 1:1).

The mechanics of this revelation are vague, though the call is concrete. Did Jonah experience God's call in a dream, a voice, or an encounter? Or, did he encounter an angelic visitor, who shared God's word with him? While we don't know the medium through which God addressed Jonah, God's instruction to Jonah is clear: "Pronounce judgment upon wicked Nineveh."

If God spoke a word to you, setting before you God's vision for your vocation, how would you respond? Would you respond gladly to God's wisdom, trusting the future to God's care, or would you try to escape God's prophetic demands?

You Can Run, but You Can't Hide. Jonah tries to do the impossible — run away from God. He buys a ticket and boards a ship, "away from the presence of the Lord." His journey begins in Joppa (Haifa), the port city of Jerusalem. No one knows the exact location of Tarshish. Some identify Tarshish with the island of Sardinia. Others believe that the Tarshish was at the edge of the earth, a Spanish sea coast port or port on the Straits of Gibraltar.

Jonah's project is bound to fail. God is not geographically limited. God is everywhere and in all things. Jonah can run, but he cannot hide from his creator. In the words of Psalm 139:

> Where can I go from your spirit? Or where can I flee from your presence? If I ascend to heaven, you are there; if I make my bed in Sheol, you are there. If I take the wings of the morning and settle at the farthest limits of the sea, even there your hand shall lead me, and your right hand shall hold me fast. (Psalm 139:7-10)

Jonah discovers the practical meaning of omnipresence: Wherever we go, God is with us.

As the apostle Paul affirmed, "Nothing can separate us from the love of God." (Romans 8:38-39). Divine love will accompany Jonah wherever he goes and regardless of what he does.

God in Nature? What happens next is just as astounding. Today, mainline and progressive Christians try to avoid anthropomorphic descriptions of God. We don't speak of God as "wrathful" or "angry" or "grieving." We are reluctant to invoke "God's will" to describe divine activity in the world. We see God moving within, but not dominating, the world. Within the intricate dynamism of cause and effect relationships, we affirm a partnership of divine and human agency. Jonah recognizes this divine-human synergy. Jonah is also clear that God is active in the world, providentially moving on land and sea. God is not outside the causal relationships of the world; nor does God intervene supernaturally out of the blue to save or destroy. Rather, God is present, the Book of Jonah suggests, in the least as well as the greatest, in the non-human as well as the human world. Nature is the theatre for divine creativity, and God can choose to be more present and active in some places than others. In Jonah's case, God "hurled a great wind upon the sea" that threatens to destroy the ship (1:4).

Could there be a divine-human synchronicity such that human behavior can elicit a divine response even in the non-human world? For Jonah and the biblical tradition, the non-human world is alive and open to divine activity. Isaiah discovers that "the whole earth is full of God's glory (Isaiah 6:1-8). The Psalmist chants, "Let everything that breathes praise God" (Psalm 150:6). Nature is alive with possibility and responds to human emotions, as Masura Emoto concludes as a result of his experiments on the impact of human emotions on water crystals.[3] According to some studies, plants also flourish or fail to thrive as a result of their emotional environment.[4]

Jonah flees God and then falls into a deep sleep. He literally shuts down in response to God's call to preach in enemy territory. Is Jonah simply disobedient or fearful of the oppressor, or does he flee from God as a result of God's heretical call to him? The possibility that his understanding of God is all wrong may be more than the prophet can take.

Pious Pagans. The author of the Book of Jonah has a surprisingly positive view of pagans or polytheists. Profoundly monotheistic in its affirmation of "the God of heaven, who made the sea and dry land" (1:9), the author is nevertheless affirmative of pagan piety. He sees a point of contact between their prayers and God's response. God is present in the storm, the fish, and the pagan. Moreover, the pagans are profoundly ethical. Despite Jonah's request to be tossed overboard, they do all they can to save him. Perhaps they are worried about spilling innocent blood. They may also have a strong ethical sense, prohibiting them from harming others without good reason. As we will see later in the text, despite their wickedness, the Ninevites can experience spiritual transformation. When they hear Jonah's message of doom, they change their lives in the hope that God will deliver them from harm. God is everywhere and in all things, and God's work in creation and human life is ultimately aimed at redemption, despite the waywardness of prophets and nations.

---

3   http://www.masaru-emoto.net/english/index.html
4   https://en.wikipedia.org/wiki/Plant_perception_%28paranormal%29

10

Grace abounds. God hears every sincere prayer and honors every deep commitment, even if such prayers and commitments are addressed to other deities. In the final pages of C.S. Lewis' *Last Battle*, Aslan encounters a follower of Aslan's demonic opponent Tash. Tash's servant expects no mercy from the victorious lion:

> Then I fell at his feet and thought, surely this is the hour of death, for the Lion (who is worthy of all honour) will know that I have served Tash all my days and not him. Nevertheless, it is better to see the Lion and die than to be Tisroc of the world and live and not to have seen him. But the Glorious One bent down his golden head and touched my forehead with his tongue and said, Son, thou art welcome. But I said, Alas, Lord, I am no son of thine but the servant of Tash. He answered, Child, all the service thou hast done to Tash, I account as service done to me.
>
> Then by reasons of my great desire for wisdom and understanding, I overcame my fear and questioned the Glorious One and said, Lord, is it then true, as the Ape said, that thou and Tash are one? The Lion growled so that the earth shook (but his wrath was not against me) and said, It is false. Not because he and I are one, but because we are opposites, I take to me the services which thou hast done to him. For I and he are of such different kinds that no service which is vile can be done to me, and none which is not vile can be done to him.
>
> Therefore if any man swear by Tash and keep his oath for the oath's sake, it is by me that he has truly sworn, though he know it not, and it is I who reward him. And if any man does a cruelty in my name, then, though he says the name Aslan, it is Tash whom he serves and by Tash his deed is accepted. Dost thou understand, Child? I said, Lord, thou knowest how much I understand. But I said also (for the truth constrained me), Yet I have been seeking Tash all my days. Beloved, said the Glorious One, unless thy desire had been for me thou shouldst not have sought so long and so truly. For all find what they truly seek."[5]

Casting Lots. A God-filled world abounds with synchronicities. Every encounter can be revelatory. Even apparently chance

5   C. S. Lewis, *The Last Battle*, (New York, Macmillian Publishing Company, 1970), 164,165.

11

events are undergirded by divine wisdom. While God is not the direct source of good and bad fortune, God's presence propels us toward positive and healing relationships. God provides nudges, intuitions, and unexpected events to guide us toward the right path. Synchronous events enable us to find a way when there is no way.

The mariners cast lots and the lot falls to Jonah. Centuries later, the author of Acts of the Apostles describes the early Christian community casting lots to determine Judas' replacement as a member of the movement's inner circle (Acts 1:23-26).

Something Fishy. Eventually the mariners acquiesce to Jonah's request and toss Jonah into the sea. They are certainly afraid, but they also may be honoring Jonah's brief moment of self-transcendence in which he is willing to die to save them. Beyond that, they are on the verge of discovering a new god, superior to the many gods they had previously worshiped.

I am sure Jonah expected to drown in the storm. God, however, has other plans for him. The One who challenges Jonah to reach out to the oppressor is willing to give Jonah another chance. God provides a large fish to swallow Jonah, thus saving his life and giving him a second opportunity to follow God's radical call. The account of the great fish is no doubt the stuff of legends. Survival for three days in a fish's stomach defies any rational explanation. The stomach juices alone, not to mention ocean depths, are fatal to any human. Still, we must remember that the Book of Jonah is not a scientific treatise, but a parable of divine patience, hospitality, and love. Facts can only take us so far on the spiritual journey. We need the graces of imagination, wonder, and amazement to save us in our own perilous journey.

God's vision is communicated to a big fish. Non-humans can be means of grace and protection. God whispers to the big fish, guiding its path to save the wayward prophet. Omnipresence leads to the possibility global revelation. Divine inspiration is not restricted to Christianity or to human beings. God seeks abundant life through diverse means. All creatures are touched by God and the higher creatures, such as this big fish, can respond to God's commands. Jonah is clear that God has a special care for the non-human world. Jonah is surely more than a big fish story; it is affirmation of God's providence, revealed in God's care for and partnership with the non-human world.

In Conclusion. Jonah is a runaway prophet. His disobedience is motivated by his religious orthodoxy. He protests against a deity whose justice is tempered by mercy and whose mercy encompasses those whose behavior merits the strictest punishment.

CHAPTER FOUR
PRAYING FROM THE DEPTHS
(JONAH 1:17-2:10)

The first chapter concludes with Jonah being swallowed by a big fish. While we don't know the species of the fish, the text recognizes that all creation is open to divine guidance. The non-human world is full of life and is often as attentive to God as humankind. In light of human caused climate change and species extinction, this is such an important point that it bears repeating as we begin our reflections on Chapter Two.

The Psalms proclaim, "Let everything that breathes praise God." (Psalm 150:6) A voice moves through the universe, eliciting praise from every creature. Perhaps, the author of the Book of Jonah recalls the majestic hymn from Psalm 148:

> Praise the LORD from the earth,
>   you sea monsters and all deeps,
> fire and hail, snow and frost,
>   stormy wind fulfilling his command!
> Mountains and all hills,
>   fruit trees and all cedars!
> Wild animals and all cattle,
>   creeping things and flying birds! (Psalm 148:7-10)

Jonah certainly encounters a sea monster, capable of doing God's bidding! God providentially moves through all things, using the movements of a great fish to deliver Jonah from certain death. From the humblest to the greatest, creation reveals God's glory. The Book of Jonah is a clear reminder that creation matters to God and has integrity and value apart from human interest.

It has been said, "Pray as you can, not as you can't." Jonah prays, but there is irony in his approach to God. Jonah gives thanks for God's deliverance. As the waves enveloped him, he called to God and God provided a great fish. Divine deliverance takes Jonah to Sheol. The prophet is alive, but barely. Perhaps, Jonah wonders what God has in mind for him as he sits in the belly of the fish. As he languishes amid the remains of the fish's most recent meal, Jonah might be praying, "Thank you, God, for saving me but get me out of this hell hole!" In the Hebraic tradition, Sheol is the place of darkness and death, almost beyond the reach of God. Yet, even in the depths God is present. Even in the darkest valley, God is with us, guiding and protecting us when we are most unaware of God's presence or have turned our backs on God's vision for our lives.

Jonah's precarious situation doesn't prevent him from pontificating. Despite his disobedience, he believes himself to be more faithful than persons of other faiths. "Those who worship vain idols forsake their true loyalty" (2:8). All too soon Jonah forgets the hospitality of the pagan mariners and their own desperate petitions for divine deliverance. God answered their prayers as well as his own. In fact, they are more in sync with God's vision than the disobedient prophet! Still, Jonah believes that his faith and ethnicity place him closer to God's heart than his heathen companions. Jonah also fails to note his own "vain idols," his own limited vision of God, disguised by the language of theological orthodoxy.

Too often believers assume that their faith, spiritual experience, or ecclesiastical traditions give them unique status in God's eyes. Just yesterday, I read a Facebook post intended to demonstrate the superiority of the Roman Catholic tradition over Protestantism. I was both amused and annoyed by the arguments cited to prove my tradition's inferior status.

For centuries, Roman Catholic theologians asserted that "outside the church, there is no salvation." Those who are denied the sacraments as a result of theological heterodoxy or lifestyle could no longer participate in the life of the church. Their souls were at risk. Not to be outdone, many conservative Protestants affirm that apart from a datable conversion experience, accompanied by the sinner's prayer, their pious neighbors are doomed to eternal darkness. They assume Roman Catholics and Orthodox Christians are idolaters as a result of their adoration of Mary the mother of Jesus. Many believers claim that if Hitler repented on his deathbed he would be saved, while damnation awaited Mahatma Gandhi because of his failure to accept Jesus Christ as his personal savior. They believe that atheists whose altruism demanded no eternal reward are spiritually inferior to Christians who accept Jesus simply to avoid the flames of hell. In contrast to such spiritual imperialism, the Book of Jonah recognizes a Godward movement in every life and honors faithfulness wherever it is found. Pagans can become pious and oppressors can forsake their violent ways.

Jonah's prayer of thanksgiving ends with a vow. When he is delivered from the belly of the fish and returns home, Jonah will sacrifice to his Creator (2:9). The text notes that pagans whose fidelity Jonah disparages also perform sacrifices in response to God's deliverance (1:16). Jonah's prayer is narcissistic and self-referential. He can't see beyond his own welfare nor can he accept the piety of outsiders. He seems to be unaware of his own disobedience.

Yet, is Jonah alone in his spiritual blindness? In times of national crisis, we pray that our enemies be defeated and ask that "God bless America" as if God has placed Iran, Syria, Palestine, North Korea, or ISIS outside the circle of divine love. We assume that God must love us more than our enemies and that God shares our blood lust for their annihilation.

Echoing Jonah's religious superiority, Mark Twain's "War Prayer" describes one preacher's patriotic supplications:

> The burden of its supplication was, that an ever-merciful and benignant Father of us all would watch over our noble young soldiers, and aid, comfort, and encourage them in their patriotic work; bless them, shield them in the day of battle and the hour of peril, bear them in His mighty hand, make them strong and confident, invincible in the bloody onset; help them to crush the foe, grant to them and to their flag and country imperishable honor and glory.

The pastor concluded with words Jonah could endorse, "Bless our arms, grant us the victory, O Lord our God, Father and Protector of our land and flag!" His prayer suggests that only our land and people matter; the sons and daughters of our nation's enemies are of no account in God's eyes.

Twain notes that as the pastor's petitions ended, a stranger walked up the aisle and challenged the congregation to reflect on the deeper meaning of such prayers for victory. "If you would beseech a blessing upon yourself, beware! lest without intent you invoke a curse upon a neighbor at the same time. If you pray for the blessing of rain upon your crop which needs it, by that act you are possibly praying for a curse upon some neighbor's crop which may not need rain and can be injured by it." The stranger continues in graphic, but challenging, words that would have met the nationalist Jonah's approval:

> O Lord our Father, our young patriots, idols of our hearts, go forth to battle — be Thou near them! With them — in spirit — we also go forth from the sweet peace of our beloved firesides to smite the foe. O Lord our God, help us to tear their soldiers to bloody shreds with our shells; help us to cover their smiling fields with the pale forms of their patriot dead; help us to drown the thunder of the guns with the shrieks of their wounded, writhing in pain; help us to lay waste their humble homes with a hurricane of fire; help us to wring the hearts of their unoffending widows with unavailing grief; help us to turn them out roofless with little children to wander unfriended the wastes of their desolated land in rags and hunger and thirst, sports of the sun flames of summer and the icy winds of winter, broken in spirit, worn with travail, imploring Thee for the refuge of the grave and denied it — for our sakes who adore Thee, Lord, blast their hopes, blight their lives, protract their bitter pilgrimage, make heavy their steps, water their way with their tears, stain the white snow with the blood of their wounded feet! We ask it, in the spirit of love, of Him Who is the Source of Love, and Who is the ever-faithful refuge and friend of all that are sore beset and seek His aid with humble and contrite hearts. Amen.[6]

If such wholesale destruction came upon Nineveh, Jonah's prayers would be answered. "Be careful what you pray for!" physician Larry Dossey counsels. You may indirectly be praying for your neighbor's harm. It is appropriate to pray for the safety of our troops and the well-being of our homeland, but we must also follow Abraham Lincoln's counsel in a time of war. "Let us not pray for God to be on our side, but that we are on God's side."

---

6 Mark Twain, *The War Prayer* (New York: Harper Colophon, 2001). Originally published in 1923.

Jonah's prayer nevertheless begs important theological and spiritual questions: Can God use our self-serving, polarizing prayers for a greater good? Is God able to purify prayers like Jonah's and our own, filled with ambivalence and emerging from our prejudice and ignorance, to support the well-being of our neighbor as well as ourselves? Honesty compels us to recognize that the Apostle Paul's confession that "all have sinned and fall short of the glory of God" applies not only to our prayer lives but also our ethics (Romans 3:23). Even our most inclusive and pious prayers must be accompanied by "Lord, have mercy upon me, a sinner!"

God hears Jonah's prayer and once again God delivers him. Disobedience cannot thwart God's grace. Jonah's "salt water taxi" hears God's whisper and in response "spewed Jonah out on dry land" (2:10). Perhaps, the great fish couldn't stomach the disobedient prophet's pious bloviating.

Jonah is grateful, but can he extend his sense of gratitude to embrace the well-being of Nineveh? Can Jonah recognize that the grace he receives, despite his disobedience, might also apply to the disobedient Nineveh?

In Conclusion. Jonah's prayers are ironic. They are also honest, reflecting his experience at the moment (2:1-9; 4:2-3). We can pray the totality of our experience, trusting that although God accepts us as we are, God never leaves us there.

CHAPTER FIVE
DELIVERED FROM DISASTER
(JONAH 3:1-10)

Once again, the word of the Lord comes to Jonah. This time he obeys. But, Jonah is still angry at God. Perhaps, he intuits that deliverance lies behind his message of doom. Deep down, he may recognize that he is no more deserving of grace than the people of Nineveh. He, too, has turned from God's way. Though he consciously denies it, he may hear God's whisper "in sighs too deep for words" emerging from the depths of the unconscious: "the love that saved you embraces your enemy as well." Still, resisting God's vision, he nevertheless secures passage on another ship and retraces his steps toward Nineveh.

Nineveh is a great city, full of hustle and bustle, and wealth and power, similar to Manhattan, Beijing, or Washington DC. "Three days walk across," the city must be legendary in size. I walk at a pace of about 3.3 miles an hour. I cover a few miles on my hour long morning walk on the Cape Cod beach near my home. If I were to walk eight hours, with a few breaks for refreshment and rest, I would cover about twenty six miles in a day. If this distance is from circumference to circumference, times three, we would be talking about a city of about 6,000 square miles, larger in area than Los Angeles, Houston, or Oklahoma City.

Words of Doom and Pleas for Mercy. Jonah's message was simple and straightforward, "Forty days more, and Nineveh shall be overthrown." As he walked from street to street, Jonah pronounced words of doom upon the city. Judgment is coming and there is no way to avoid it. The threat is real and imminent. The impact is catalytic. Jonah only needs to walk a third of the distance across Nineveh for his message to take hold. Perhaps, at first, he is seen as another "nut case," but as day progresses the people go from denial to anger and hopelessness and then the desperate hope that God's judgment can be averted.

19

Unlike the majority of persons in our nation, who believe global climate change is gradual and incremental and can be forestalled by turning off a few lights and recycling, the people of Nineveh see the impact of God's judgment as inexorable and immediate in nature. There is no time to waste. Survival demands an immediate change of heart and a transformation of behavior. From king to peasant, the city must change direction, forsake wickedness, and throw itself on God's mercy. The Ninevites anxiously yearn for deliverance: "Perhaps — and there is no guarantee — God will turn aside from God's vision, the impact of our actions will be blunted, and our repentance will avert disaster." Hoping against hope, the citizens of Nineveh desperately depend on God's mercy. Relying on grace alone, they cast their future upon a deity they barely know.

As I ponder the call and response described in the Book of Jonah, I am reminded of a hymn I often heard during my childhood. At revival meetings held at my childhood Baptist church, the sermon was always followed by an altar call, inviting sinners to trust God alone for their salvation, knowing that only God, and not our goodness, can save us from unbelief and sin. We trusted the scriptural promise that "all who call upon the name of God will be saved" (Romans 10:13).

1. Just as I am, without one plea,
but that thy blood was shed for me,
and that thou bidst me come to thee,
O Lamb of God, I come, I come.
2. Just as I am, and waiting not
to rid my soul of one dark blot,
to thee whose blood can cleanse each spot,
O Lamb of God, I come, I come.
3. Just as I am, though tossed about
with many a conflict, many a doubt,
fightings and fears within, without,
O Lamb of God, I come, I come.
4. Just as I am, poor, wretched, blind;
sight, riches, healing of the mind,
yea, all I need in thee to find,
O Lamb of God, I come, I come.

Just as they are, the Ninevites plead for divine mercy. They have nothing to bring to God, for their wickedness is great. They simply cling to hope for salvation from a "love unknown [which] hath broken every barrier down."

The Pathway of Repentance. The people of Nineveh change their ways. The king calls for a fast that will embrace the whole community:

> No human being or animal, no herd or flock, shall taste anything. They shall not feed, nor shall they drink water. Human beings and animals shall be covered with sackcloth and they shall cry mightily to God. All shall turn from their evil ways and the violence that is in their hands. (3:7-8)

Threat turns to repentance on a political as well as personal level. In spite of his hardheartedness, Jonah's unsympathetic call reflects the spirit of the prophetic tradition. Nations must change their hearts and turn away from the pathways of death to embrace God's vision of Shalom, justice, equality, and hospitality.

Contrast for a moment, our political response to the terrorist attacks on September 11, 2001. Instead of reflecting prayerfully on our nation's foreign policy and its role in provoking attacks, we turned immediately to restoring life as it was before 9/11. We were urged to travel and go shopping as a way of defeating the terrorists. Our leaders called for retaliation. No one spoke of repentance. There is no doubt that justice needed to be done. Osama bin Laden and his followers needed to be defeated. Still, what would have happened if we as a nation had cried out for divine mercy and wisdom? What would have happened in the conduct of our nation's foreign policy if we had acknowledged that we also commit violence in the Middle East? What would have happened to our national spirit if the President proclaimed a fast and asked for the nation to pray for divine forgiveness for policies that lead to violence?

I raise these questions, not as pacifist, but as one who believes that we need a strong and pragmatic national defense policy. Still, I am sure the Hebraic prophets, including the ambivalent Jonah, would have called our nation's leaders to prayerful reflection. They would have invited us as a nation to seek justice and equity in our homeland as well as in foreign policy.

The Great "Perhaps." The king and the citizens of Nineveh remain uncertain about the future. Perhaps, they recognize that their immorality and oppression has sown the seeds of the city's destruction. Like Jonah, they may believe that if the city is destroyed, they are only getting what they deserve. Yet, there is hope that God will respond to the sinner's call and that a lifetime of wickedness can be transformed by divine mercy. With a quivering voice, I suspect, the king addresses the nation:

> Who knows? God may relent and change his mind; he
> may turn from his fierce anger so that we do not perish. (3:9)

While I do not believe in the linear acts-consequences theology, enshrined in Deuteronomy 28, and challenged by the Book of Job, it is clear that our acts have consequences. Injustice leads to unrest. Consumerism and the rampant use of fossil fuels are factors in global climate change. Oppression sows the seeds of revolution. Unfair tax and governmental policies lead to widening the gap between the wealthiest 1% and the majority of Americans. Indeed, turning from God and focusing on our own well-being may lead, as the prophet Amos proclaims, to a famine of hearing God's word (Amos 8:11). Grace is more powerful than sin, and can be catalytic in the healing of persons and nations; but we cannot assume grace. We must throw ourselves upon the grace of God, crying out, "Lord, have mercy upon me a sinner," and trust, even in our feelings of hopelessness, that our repentance opens a door for new possibilities of personal and social transformation.

God Changes! Transforming God and Transforming Theology. What happens next astounds the Ninevites, Jonah, and proponents of orthodox theology throughout the ages. Listen carefully, letting these words soak in. They could change your life and your understanding of God.

> When God saw what they did, how they changed their
> evil ways, God changed his mind about the calamity he had
> said he would bring upon them; and he did not do it. (3:10; see
> also Exodus 32: 12, 14; Amos 7:3.6; Jeremiah 18:7-11, 26:2-3)

"God changed God's mind." God altered God's course. God freely changed.

God's plans. While this does not constitute a complete theology, God's response tells us something important about God's relationship to history and our daily lives: The future is not pre-destined nor is God's plan or knowledge eternal and unchanging. God is alive, historical, and constantly able to change to adapt to a changing world or initiate new saving possibilities. God's love is non-negotiable, but love's expressions are always relative to time and place. As Lamentations proclaims:

> The steadfast love of the Lord never ceases, God's mercies never come to an end; they are new every morning; great is your faithfulness. (Lamentations 3:22-23)

In the following paragraphs, I will invite you to join me on a theological journey, exploring the meaning of God's knowledge, power, and presence in light of the Book of Jonah. Theologians often describe God in terms of the "omni" words — omnipresent, omnipotent (or omni-active), and omniscient. Despite the abstract explanations of many theologians which render these words incomprehensible to most laypersons, the practical meaning of these words can be a matter of faith and unfaith and life and death. It certainly was in the case of the Ninevites.

As I was driving my grandson to kindergarten recently, he stated that "infinity plus infinity is infinity" and then added "God is more than infinity." In his own youthful way, he captured the deeper meaning of the "omni" words utilized by theologians and laypersons alike. First, God is omnipresent. When I asked an adult faith formation class at church what the word "omnipresence means," they responded with: "God is everywhere," "Wherever I go, God is with me," "I'm always in God's care." When Isaiah encounters the Holy One in the Jerusalem Temple, the cherubim and seraphim proclaim, "The whole earth is full of God's glory" (Isaiah 6:1-8). Paul asserts, employing the wisdom of non-Christian philosophers, that God is the reality "in whom we live and move and have our being" (Acts 17:28). Though Jonah tries to run away from God, he runs right into God's hands. In the depths of Sheol, divine providence is at work to guide and protect Jonah and us. Omnipresence means that God is fully present in the Jerusalem Temple, among God's chosen people, in the lives of the pagan mariners, in the domestic beasts of Nineveh, in the great fish, and among the oppressive Ninevites. The intensity of God's presence is variable and God's care is always personal. Still, divine providence shapes every situation and person.

Practically, speaking the doctrine of omnipresence affirms that God is present in our enemies as well as our friends. What does it mean to say that God is present — the divine image alive, despite our turning from it — in every person, including the ISIS terrorist, the addict on the street corner, the protester blocking entrance to Planned Parenthood, and us? Divine presence is not neutral, however. As Jonah discovers, God's providential presence is always characterized by love and mercy.

God is omniscient. When we discussed the meaning of omniscience in the same adult faith formation class, the participants responded with: "God knows everything," "God knows the past, present, and future,' "Whatever happens, God is aware of it." Many theologians claim that long before the world was created, God knew everything that was to occur. They believe that past, present, and future are held in an eternal now. Nothing can be added or subtracted to God's perfect knowledge of the universe. While it can be reassuring to know that God knows every future actuality for us and our loved ones, the Book of Jonah suggests another possibility. "God changed God's mind." God changed the script in real time, in the rough and tumble world of history, to respond to the Ninevites' repentance.

Scripture is clear that God's knowledge is complete. It is not so clear about the extent of divine foreknowledge. What matters theologically and spiritually is that God knows us completely and loves us fully. "Search me and know me," Psalm 139 proclaims. The Psalmist recognized how important it is for someone to know us and despite their knowledge, to fully accept and care about us. A god who knows us in real time, as each moment of life emerges, feels our pain and experiences our joy. New knowledge opens up the possibility for new interventions on God's part. God experiences something new — the humans and their animals of Nineveh repent — that leads to a new and decisive response on God's part.

Omnipotence is traditionally related to God's sovereign and providential activity in every moment of life. When I asked an adult

24

study how they understood divine omnipotence, the responses were also varied: "God determines everything that occurs," "God's providence shapes our lives," "God does whatever God can to help us." My congregants and I struggle, nevertheless, with the implications of a God who determines everything that occurs. Does that mean that God causes cancer and car accidents? Did God cause the terrorists to attack the World Trade Center? Is God the source of evil as well as good? A god who can do everything can be reassuring, especially in uncertain times. From this perspective, nothing happens without God's permission or decision. God will defeat the forces of evil. Still, a god who is defined primarily by power rather than love is, from our vantage point, morally ambiguous.

In contrast to theological positions that define power as unilateral and coercive, I believe that God's power is relational and supportive. I believe that although God is powerful, the alpha and omega, the beginning and end of all things, God's power is ultimately loving power and that love must include faithful as well as infidel, oppressor as well as oppressed. "God is love," proclaims I John 4:8. John 3:16 affirms: "For God so loved the world that [God] gave [God's] only begotten son." God's loving power encourages human freedom and creativity.

When we respond faithfully to God's prevenient, or prior, grace, God is able to do more in our lives than if we turned away. Indeed, when Jonah proclaims "Forty days more, and Nineveh shall be overthrown," God may be experiencing the same uncertainty as the King of Nineveh. As God hears the prophet's message, perhaps, God also wonders, "Who knows? Perhaps the people of Nineveh will relent from their evil and change their minds, and experience my love." In response to Nineveh's repentance, God gives the Ninevites and Jonah, if he only opens his heart, more than they can ask or imagine.

Throughout the text, Jonah's main problem with God is that God is merciful and that God's love extends even to the people of Nineveh and their domestic animals. Jonah is so upset by God's mercy that he fails to remember, as the Letter of John was later to affirm, "Whoever does not love does not know God, for God is love" (I John 4:8). Somehow we must follow the counsel to "love your enemies and pray for those who persecute you" (Matthew 5:44). Still, we ask, "Can such injunctions apply to the terrorist, the political foe, the nasty neighbor, or the naysayer at church?" Jonah can affirm "you shall love your neighbor but hate your enemy." The idea of loving your enemy, even if God requires it, is beyond his comprehension, and so he flees from God both physically and spiritually.

In Conclusion. Theology matters! It can shape foreign policy, the justice system, congregational decision-making, and relationships in our family and neighborhood. If, as the Book of Jonah suggests, what we do matters to God and shapes God's decisions, then we want to insure that our decisions enable God to be more active and effective in saving our world. The great "perhaps," articulated in the Book of Jonah, applies to our relationship with God. "Perhaps" we will forsake our warring ways and find peace in the Middle East. "Perhaps" we will reform our economics so that "justice rolls down like waters and righteousness like an everlasting stream (Amos 5:24). "Perhaps" we will change our lifestyles and economics and avert the catastrophe of global climate change. We and God can only hope and pray!

CHAPTER SIX
A WIDENESS IN GOD'S MERCY?
(JONAH 4:1-11)

You'd think that Jonah would be happy. A whole city has been saved from devastation. But, despite the success of his message, he's angrier than ever. No doubt, he hated the Ninevites, but his real anger is directed against God for changing the rules of the theological game. In reaching out to save Nineveh, God shatters Jonah's world view. Jonah believes that goodness should be rewarded and evil punished without exception, and when God changes God's mind, the moral order of the universe, at least the order he lived by, collapses. As he looks at the plight of Israel, Jonah can't imagine Nineveh receiving God's mercy while God's chosen ones must live with poverty, insecurity, and political instability. Jonah's viewpoint is similar to that of the early Christian theologian who suggested that one of the joys of heaven is hearing the torments of the damned and feeling grateful that we have escaped their fate.

What can Jonah believe if that God's way is entirely different from what he previously lived by? As the foundations of his theological world view collapse, Jonah can't take it anymore. He would rather die than live in a world in which the wicked receive grace and God's chosen ones struggle.

Jonah, Job, and the Iconoclastic God. In many ways, the books of Jonah and Job are the most theologically radical texts in the Hebraic scriptures in their attempt to fathom the mysterious and theologically earth-shaking acts of God. Like the Book of Jonah, the Book of Job presents a theological world view in crisis. Job, the most righteous person on earth, suddenly and without prior warning or any discernible reason, loses everything — health, children, wealth, and status in the community. Job had always believed in the moral calculus, described in Deuteronomy 28: the righteous prosper and the evil cursed. But, now Job is among the cursed.

Job cries out to God, and initially all he receives is sheer silence. Even Job's friends turn against him, accusing him eventually of being the worst of sinners. Their accusations, like Jonah's anger, are self-interested. If the one person who is, to all appearances, most righteous falls from grace, then their lives are at risk. They too might lose everything. Somehow Job must deserve his misery.[7]

In both texts, God is the ultimate iconoclast, absolutely free to contradict our theological and ethical visions without prior notice. Can we trust the universe and its creator if the good suffer and the evil prosper, the enemy saved and the friend abandoned? What's the point of accepting Jesus as your savior if non-Christians are saved as well?

Both books invite us to look more deeply into reality. God's providence and mercy are greater than we can imagine. We live in an ambiguous universe, without guarantees, but God is faithful, despite all appearances. Several centuries after Jonah was penned, Jesus proclaimed, to the chagrin of the righteous, "Just so, I tell you, there will be more joy in heaven over one sinner who repents than over ninety nine righteous who need no repentance" (Luke 15:7).

A Person of Prayer? In many ways, the Book of Jonah is a treatise on the divine-human relationship. The pagan mariners and the king of Nineveh cry out to God. Jonah hears God's call and even great fish, domestic animals, and lowly worms have personal relations with their creator.

Chapter Four begins with Jonah bearing his heart once more to the God of land and sea. Jonah is angry, for God has once more disappointed the prophet. Imagine being disappointed by grace and mercy, and yet Jonah is! He wants retribution and wrath. He wants hell-fire and brimstone to descend on Nineveh. Like many who expect Jesus' Second Coming, he goes to the edge of the city, presumably to view from a safe distance God's scorched earth policy in action!

In the spirit of the Psalms, Jonah prays his anger. "O Lord! Is not this what I said when I was in my own country? This is why I fled to Tarshish at the beginning" (4:2). Jonah is protesting God's deliverance of wicked Nineveh. The god that he believed in would have destroyed these heathens without remorse.

---

7 For more on Job, see Bruce Epperly, *Finding God in Suffering: A Journey with Job* (Gonzales, FL: Energion, 2014).

Jonah continues with words that betray his own failure to understand God or himself. With more than a hint of irony, the text continues, "For I know that you are a gracious God, merciful and slow to anger, and abounding in steadfast love, and ready to relent from punishing" (4:2). Jonah has experienced divine mercy. He doesn't deserve grace, according to his theological viewpoint. God is sovereign and, even if his disobedience was warranted, he deserves nothing from the king. Yet, God sends a fish to spare him and willingly restores his prophetic mantle. Jonah is no doubt sincere, but he cannot accept the scandalous wideness of God's mercy. God delivered sinful Jonah and nurtured wayward Israel. Wouldn't God also take the initiative in delivering the sinful city of Nineveh from destruction?

Job goes so far as to pray for his own death. He can't abide mercy that embraces enemy as well as friend. He wants vengeance. He knows that although God has forgiven his sin, he can't tolerate God's forgiving Nineveh. Jonah thumbs his nose at God and says he'd rather die than live in such an ethically unfair universe.

Sacred Questions. In the final chapter, God responds to Jonah with questions rather than answers or admonitions. Often the best teaching and pastoral care comes as the result of provocative questions that draw us out and reveal our blind spots without putting us on the defensive. While God can be direct, God is more often subtle, influencing our lives through apparently chance encounters, persisting questions, gentle insights, and comments from companions. Every encounter can be revelatory, exposing our deepest motives and providing insights into God's providential activity.

God's first question comes in response to Jonah's angry and self-serving prayer. "Is it right for you to be angry?" As angry as he is at God, Jonah entirely misses the point of God's question. In fact, he doesn't respond at all.

God often has to deal with humankind's hard-hearted and hardheadedness. God's relationship with Jonah is no exception to God's patient luring of humankind from parochialism to globalism and self-interest to world loyalty. The point of God's questions, I believe, is "Wake up and smell the coffee, Jonah. Get some perspective. How can you be angry when a great city is spared from disaster?"

Jonah reflects our own narrow theologies, revealed in our rejoicing at the ill-fortune of others and demise of our enemies. When I heard the news of Osama bin Laden's death at the hands of USA Special Forces, I pumped my fist in joy. When a natural disaster strikes on foreign soil, I often breathe a sigh of relief. Despite the fact that they are God's beloved children, created in God's image, the death of ISIS and al Qaeda leaders becomes an occasion for celebration.

Jonah flees town, unable to tolerate the Ninevites' prayers of gratitude. He erects a shelter from the sun, hoping that God will repent of his decision to save Nineveh. But, Jonah is sorely disappointed. The day grows hotter and Jonah grows more depressed at God's failure to punish Nineveh.

Despite his anger and alienation, God doesn't give up on Jonah. In fact, he provides the disappointed prophet a vine to give him comfort against sun and heat. Jonah is beside himself with joy! The vine, no doubt, is intended as a teaching moment, inviting Jonah to expand his understanding of grace to include the Ninevites. Still, Jonah doesn't get it.

Jonah's elation is temporary. A worm, appointed by God, attacked the bush, rendering Jonah defenseless against heat and wind. Once again, Jonah cries out to God, "It is better to die than live," inspiring God to ask his second question, "Is it right for you to be angry about the bush?" God is still trying to get Jonah to see life from a wider perspective. "Yes, Jonah, you are uncomfortable. But, you are still alive and so are the people of Nineveh!" Jonah remains recalcitrant. "Yes, I have a right to be angry. I'm angry enough to die!"

God never gives up on us or on Jonah. God first makes an observation and then asks a third question, "You are concerned about the bush, for which you did not labor and which you did not grow; it came into being in a night and perished in a night. And should I not be concerned about Nineveh, that great city, in which there are more than a hundred and twenty thousand persons who

30

do not know their right hand from their left, and also many animals?" (4:10-11).

God wants Jonah to know that everything is grace. None of us is self-made. We depend on a constellation of relationships for our well-being. Even the growth of a bush is a miracle grounded in God's wise creativity along with soil and water. Each human, including a disobedient prophet, is a miracle. God challenges Jonah's self-centeredness, "Ninevite lives matter! They are created in my image. They've turned from me, but there's hope for them and there's hope for you. Open your heart. You can change, too!"

In Conclusion. The Book of Jonah ends with a question, "Shouldn't I, God, be concerned about Nineveh and its domestic animals?" We have no idea how Jonah responded. Did he drag himself back home, angry or depressed? Or, did he have an epiphany, a change of heart, and move from nationalism to globalism, from alienation to love?

Today, that same question is asked of us. We see the bodies of Syrian children on Mediterranean beaches. Cable news reports terrorist massacres and the destruction of sacred sites. Politicians vie with one another about who can be most xenophobic and efficient in deporting undocumented workers. African American teenagers fear walking on the streets, worried not only about gangs, but also police violence. Global climate change threatens coastal areas like my home on Cape Cod, animal species, and human life as a whole. Like the Book of Jonah, our future is open. How will we respond?

CHAPTER SEVEN
JONAH'S WORD FOR US

Jonah invites us to an adventure of the spirit that is theological and ethical. When we want to create a god who reflects our own cultural and religious biases, isolating ourselves from other religions, cultures, and ethnicities, God breaks through our small-mindedness, overturning our theological certainties and inviting us to a larger landscape of love.

While our understanding of scripture can never fully determine public policy in a democratic society, Jonah invites us to expand our ethical horizons. When are tempted to prejudicial and xenophobic actions, the Book of Jonah challenges us to remember: Ninevite lives matter! Syrian lives matter! Black lives matter! All lives matter! God's circle includes everyone, even our enemies. As poet Edwin Markham (1852-1940) penned:

> He drew a circle that shut me out –
> Rebel, heretic, thing to flout.
> But love and I had the wit to win:
> We drew a circle that took him in.

Jonah invites us to affirm the mystic affirmation, "God is a circle whose center is everywhere and whose circumference is nowhere." Everyone is in God's circle. Even when we must mete out justice, we must remember that those whom we oppose are also God's children. Their lives and deaths matter to God. We should mourn rather than celebrate the deaths of our enemies.

Jonah invites us to look for God's presence in persons of other faiths and no explicit faith at all. Our faith is a matter of awareness and not superiority. Jonah inspires us to look for expressions of spirituality, moral goodness, and piety among "secular" persons.

Jonah challenges us to expand our ethical consciousness to include the non-human world. The text is clear that the animal kingdom matters to God. Further, God speaks within non-human experience, the great fish and the domestic animals, inspiring them to do God's bidding. Plants and natural phenomena reflect divine wisdom and creativity. Care for the earth, faithful readers of the book of Jonah discover, is a mandate and not optional. When earth stands in the balance, our calling is to be God's partners in healing the world, letting go of self-interest and committing ourselves to world loyalty. This is the message of Jonah: God loves the world and all its habitants, and our calling is to love the world as well.

GROUP STUDY QUESTIONS

Jonah is an imaginative text. Faithfulness to Jonah inspires us to read and respond imaginatively, looking for God-moments in our own lives and exploring where our ethics and theological have stood in the way of fidelity to God. We may not flee to Tarshish, but we escape God's call in other, often culturally and socially acceptable ways.

As a prelude to each session, take a few minutes for silent prayer, inviting God to turn upside down our prejudices and awaken us to a wider vision of grace for us, our neighbors, strangers, and enemies.

SESSION ONE

Focus: Jonah 1:1-17
Read: *Jonah*, Chapters I-III

1) What is your understanding of scripture? Should we affirm every word of scripture as factual? Or does scripture involve legend, myth, and poetry? If Jonah was a purely fictional character, would it make any difference to you?

2) The United Church of Christ affirms that "God is still speaking." Do you think God does new things and changes God's mind on ethical issues in response to changing situations? Do you think different social and historical settings challenge us to revise our theology and ethics, for example, in relationship to religious pluralism, sexuality, end of life ethics?

3) What motivates Jonah to run away from God? How would you respond if it appeared that God asked you to do something, or believe something, contrary to what you previously knew about God's intention for you or the world?

4) What do you think of the phrase "The Bible says it. I believe it. And that settles it?"

5) Take a moment to imagine God's "word" to Jonah. What do you think happened? Do you think God really "speaks" to people? Do you think such revelations are "pure" or that

they are received in terms of our own cultural, religious, and historical context?

6) How would you describe the pagan mariners? Can non-Christians, polytheists (like the mariners), or atheists be ethical? Do you think God uses "non-believers" in positive ways?

7) How do you respond to C.S. Lewis' description of piety from unbelievers? "Therefore if any man swear by Tash and keep his oath for the oath's sake, it is by me that he has truly sworn, though he know it not, and it is I who reward him."

8) Do you think God is at work in the natural world shaping natural events? Can God initiate a storm, or are such comments strictly legendary?

9) The Book of Jonah describes God directing the movements of a large fish. Do you think God communicates with non-humans? Do you think non-humans can respond to God?

SESSION TWO

Focus: Jonah 1:17-2:10
Read: *Jonah,* Chapter IV

1) What do you think of Jonah's prayer? Do you see the prayer as ironical in nature?

2) Imagine what it would be like to be in the belly of a fish for three days. What would it be like?

3) A leader of a major denomination asserted that God doesn't hear the prayers of non-Christians. How do you respond to his judgment on God's relationship with non-Christians?

4) How do we discern the truth claims of religious traditions? Is truth entirely relative or are some traditions more authentic than others? How do you discern the truth of competing religious traditions?

5) What do you think of persons who claim to hold "orthodox" Christian positions? Is there one "orthodoxy" or many paths to God?

6) How do you respond to the statement "the Book of Jonah recognizes a Godward movement in every life and honors faithfulness wherever it is found?"

35

7) Take a moment to re-read Mark Twain's "War Prayer" (warprayer.org). In what ways does Twain's account challenge public religious statements or prayers? Is it legitimate to affirm "God bless America?" Does this statement exclude God blessing other lands and peoples?
8) How do you evaluate the following: Abraham Lincoln's counsel in a time of war. "Let us not pray for God to be on our side, but that we are on God's side?"
9) Imagine you are the great fish. How did you feel to have Jonah in your belly? Were you relieved when you finally vomited him out?

SESSION THREE

Focus: Jonah 3:1-10
Read: *Jonah*, Chapter V
1) Why do you think that Jonah finally obeyed God and went to Nineveh? What was his motivation to obey God this time?
2) If you were asked to be a prophet to a particular group, which group would be most difficult to you? Would you be tempted to run away from God?
3) If a prophet were to speak of impending doom for your nation, what wickedness would this prophet cite?
4) Following 9/11, do you think the USA should have, like Nineveh, entered a time of prayer, fasting, confession, and repentance for our national sins?
5) The book of Jonah reports that the King of Nineveh made the following decree: No human being or animal, no herd or flock, shall taste anything. They shall not feed, nor shall they drink water. Human beings and animals shall be covered with sackcloth and they shall cry mightily to God. All shall turn from their evil ways and the violence that is in their hands (3:7-8). What do you think of this decree? Can animals "repent?"
6) Do you think the future is open and undecided for God and us? Do you think God can experience new things and in response "change" God's mind?

7) Do you think humans have a role as God's companions in healing the world? Does God "need" us to support God's vision of Shalom, justice, and peace?

SESSION FOUR

Focus: Jonah 4:1-11
Read: *Jonah,* Chapters V and VI
1) God asks Job three questions in the final chapter. In what ways, is asking questions helpful? How can insightful questions change our lives?
2) Job believes God is merciful but can't imagine this mercy extending to Nineveh. Who might you place outside God's mercy? Do you think God provides second chances for us?
3) Is it possible to forfeit divine mercy? What actions might exclude God's mercy?
4) How would you evaluate Jonah's prayer life? Do you think God accepts "theologically inappropriate" prayers such as Jonah's? Can we share our anger with God?
5) What lesson might Jonah have learned from the shade plant — its growth and death?
6) Does God care for the non-human world? Are non-human species valuable apart from human interests?
7) Fill in the blank: "Shouldn't I, God, be concerned about _____?" What inspired you to list this group?
8) Take a moment to write a conclusion to the Book of Jonah. How did Jonah eventually respond?
9) What was your greatest learning from reading the Book of Jonah?

HELPFUL TEXTS

Miguel de la Torre, *Liberating Jonah: Forming an Ethic of Reconciliation*. New York: Maryknoll, 2007.

Bruce Epperly, *Hosea, Joel, Amos, Obadiah, Jonah*. Nashville: Abingdon Press, 2013.

Bruce Epperly, *Finding God in Suffering: A Journey with Job*. Gonzalez, FL: Energion Publications, 2014.

Bruce Epperly, *Process Theology: Embracing Adventure with God*. Gonzalez, FL: Energion Publications, 2014.

Terence E. Fretheim. *The Message of Jonah: A Theological Commentary*. Eugene, OR: Wipf and Stock, 2000.

TOPICAL LINE DRIVES

Straight to the Point in under 44 Pages

All Topical Line Drives volumes are priced at $5.99 print and $2.99 in all e-book formats.

Available

The Authority of Scripture in a Postmodern Age: Some Help from Karl Barth
Robert D. Cornwall
The Authorship of Hebrews: The Case for Paul — David Alan Black
The Caregiver's Beattitudes — Robert Martin
Constructing Your Testimony — Doris Horton Murdoch
The Eucharist: Encounters with Jesus at the Table — Robert D. Cornwall
Forgiveness: Finding Freedom from Your Past — Harvey Brown, Jr.
From Here to Eternity: Preparing for the Next Great Adventure
Rendering unto Caesar — Chris Surber
Holistic Spirituality: Life Transforming Wisdom from the Letter of James
Bruce Epperly
I'm Right and You're Wrong — Steve Kindle
Pathways to Prayer — David Moffett-Moore
Process Theology: Embracing Adventure with God — Bruce Epperly
Rendering unto Caesar — Chris Surber
Ruth & Esther: Women of Agency and Adventure — Bruce Epperly
Stewardship: God's Way of Recreating the World — Steve Kindle
To Date or Not to Date: What the Bible Says about Pre-Marital Relationships
D. Kevin Brown
What is Wrong with Social Justice — Elgin Hushbeck, Jr.
What Protestants Need to Know about Roman Catholics — Robert LaRochelle
What Roman Catholics Need to Know about Protestants — Robert LaRochelle
Why Christians Should Care about Their Jewish Roots — Nancy Petrey

Forthcoming

God the Creator: The Variety of Christian Views on Origins — Henry Neufeld
A Cup of Cold Water — Chris Surber
Understanding Textual Criticism — Thomas Hudgins

Generous Quantity Discounts Available
Dealer Inquiries Welcome
Energion Publications — P.O. Box 841
Gonzalez, FL 32560
Website: http://energionpubs.com
Phone: (850) 525-3916

Finding God in Suffering
A Journey with Job

Bruce G. Epperly

... [W]ise, honest, and liberating.

—Patricia Adams Farmer
Author of *Embracing a Beautiful God*

ALSO BY BRUCE EPPERLY

In this brief, lively, and engaging book, Dr. Bruce Epperly untangles the difficult concepts of process theology and shows how we can envision a God who is in relation to us throughout our lives here and in the next world.

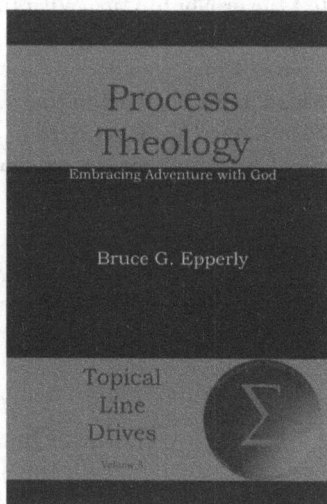

Process
Theology

Embracing Adventure with God

Bruce G. Epperly

Topical
Line
Drives

Σ